EASY PIANO

Christian Songs for Children

Visit Hal Leonard Online at
www.halleonard.com

ISBN 978-0-634-01278-5

HAL•LEONARD®
CORPORATION
7777 W. BLUEMOUND RD. P.O. BOX 13819 MILWAUKEE, WI 53213

Visit Hal Leonard Online at
www.halleonard.com

Christian Songs for Children

ALL NIGHT, ALL DAY

Spiritual

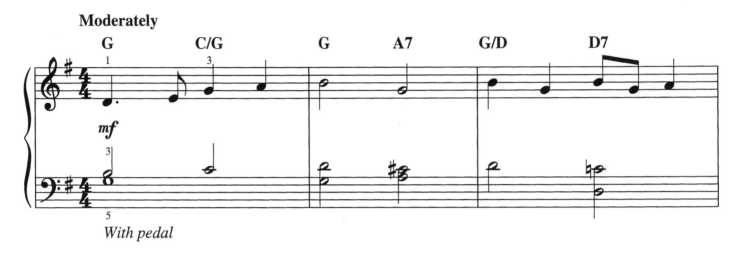

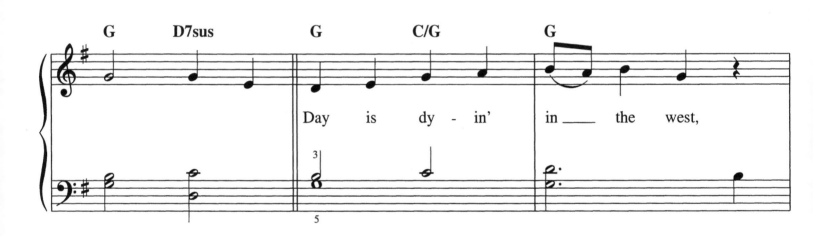

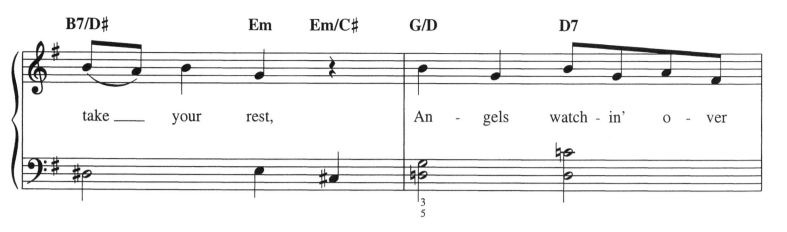

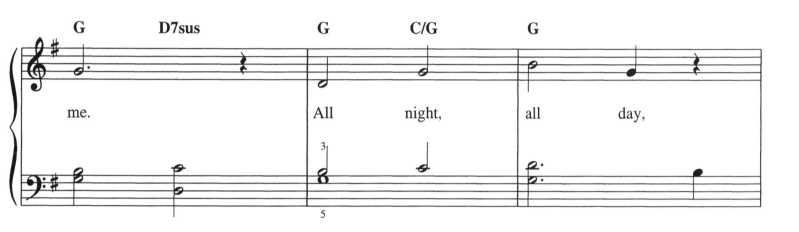

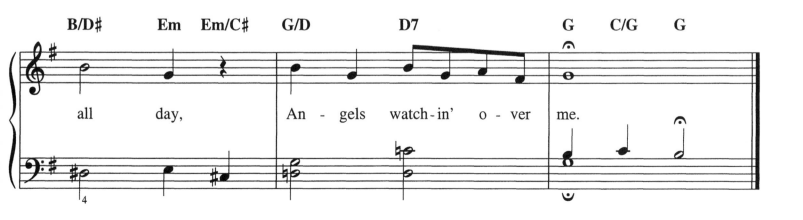

ARKY, ARKY

Traditional

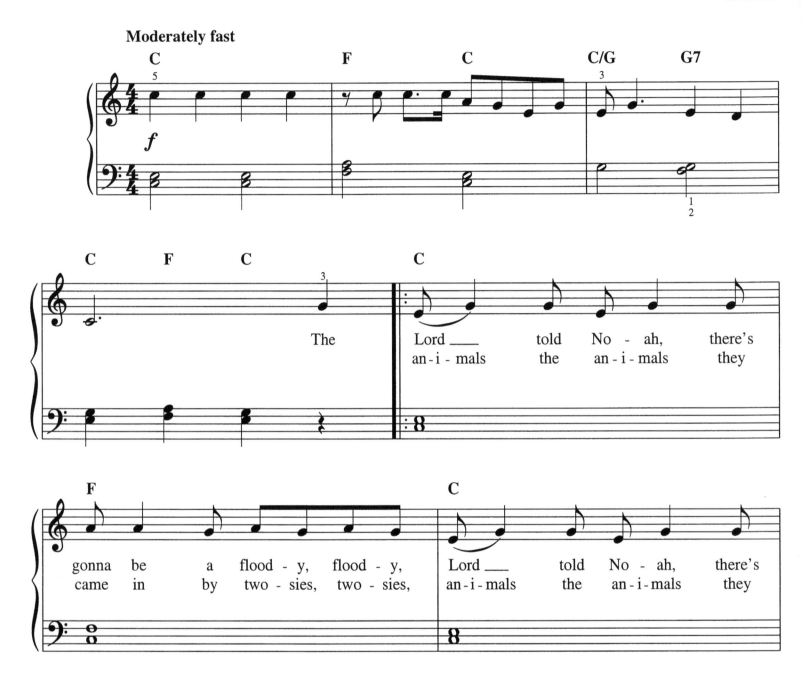

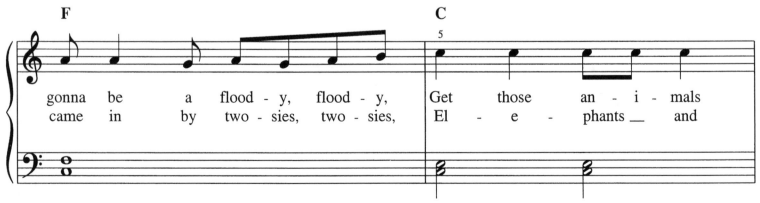

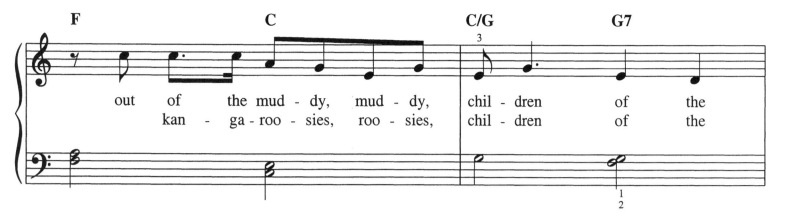

out of the mud - dy, mud - dy, chil - dren of the
kan - ga-roo - sies, roo - sies, chil - dren of the

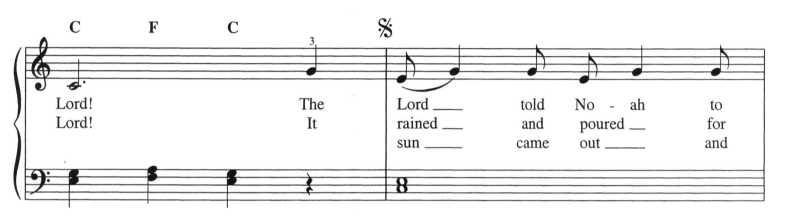

Lord! The Lord ___ told No - ah to
Lord! It rained ___ and poured ___ for
sun ___ came out ___ and

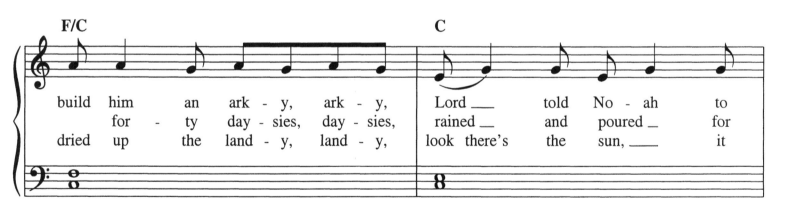

build him an ark - y, ark - y, Lord ___ told No - ah to
for - ty day - sies, day - sies, rained ___ and poured ___ for
dried up the land - y, land - y, look there's the sun, ___ it

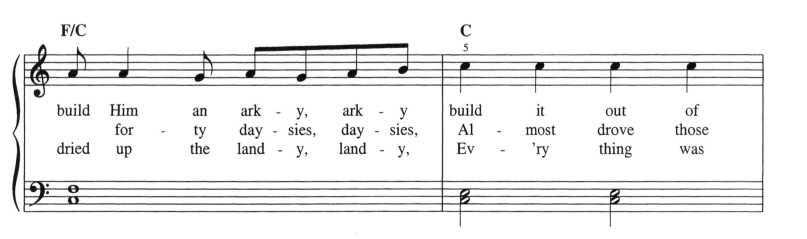

build Him an ark - y, ark - y build it out of
for - ty day - sies, day - sies, Al - most drove those
dried up the land - y, land - y, Ev - 'ry thing was

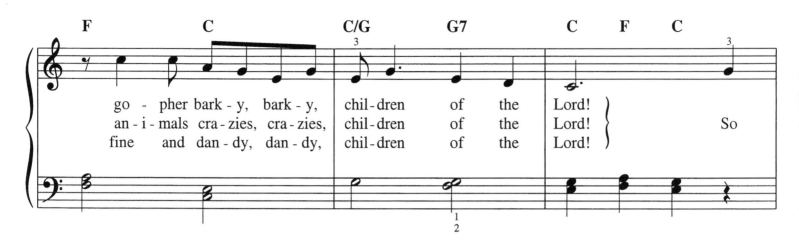

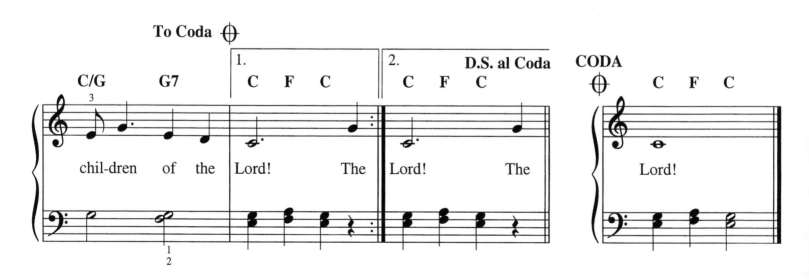

THE B-I-B-L-E

Traditional

DEEP AND WIDE

Traditional

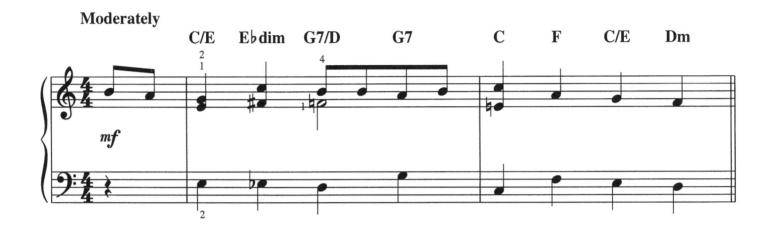

Deep   and wide,   deep   and wide, there's a   foun - tain   flow-ing deep and

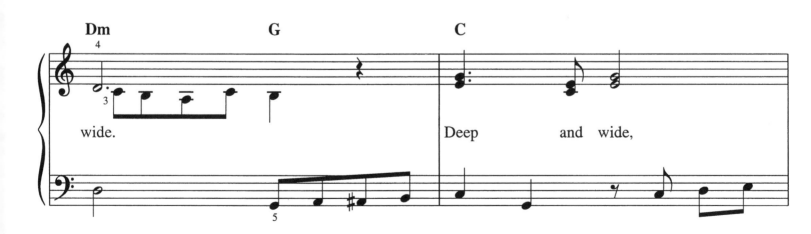

wide.   Deep   and   wide,

DO LORD

Traditional

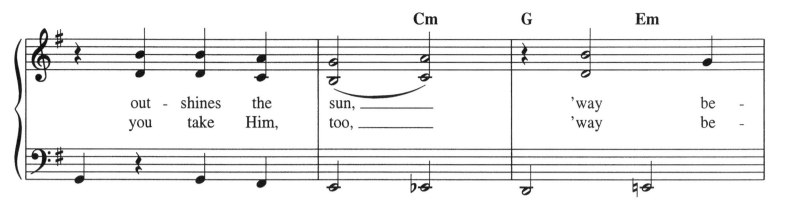

out - shines the sun, _____ 'way be -
you take Him, too, _____ 'way be -

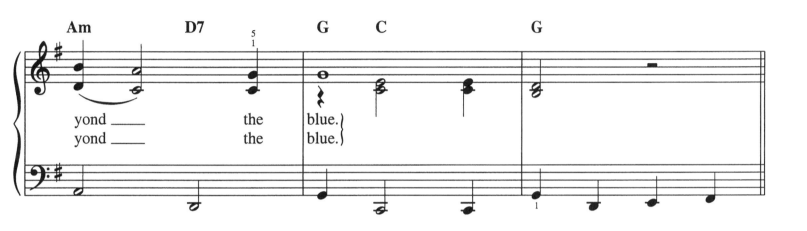

yond ____ the blue.)
yond ____ the blue.)

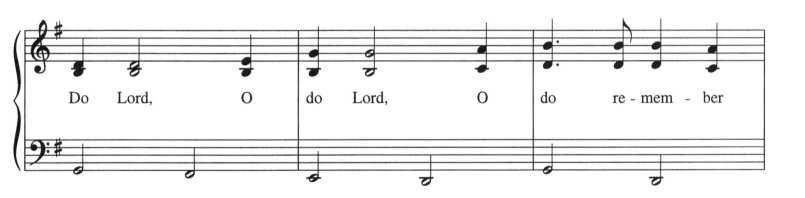

Do Lord, O do Lord, O do re - mem - ber

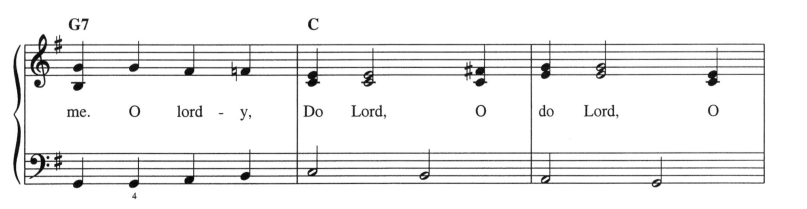

me. O lord - y, Do Lord, O do Lord, O

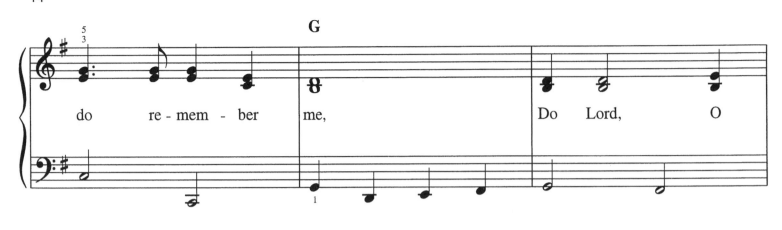

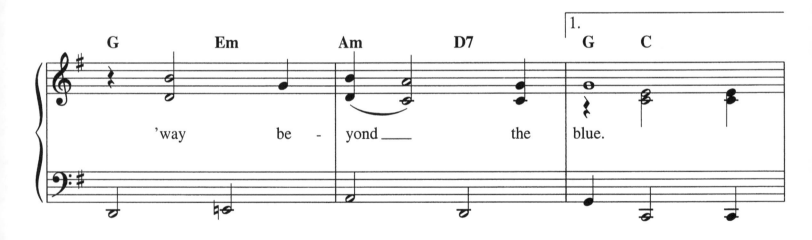

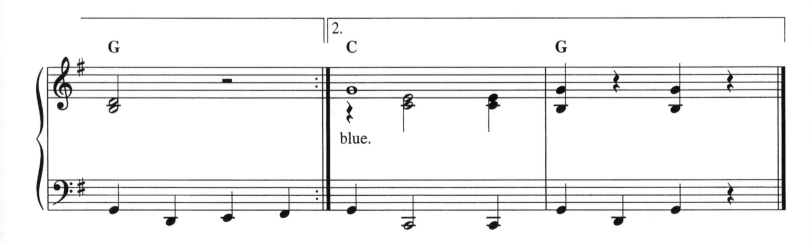

DOWN IN MY HEART

Traditional

joy,   joy,   joy,   joy,   down   in   my

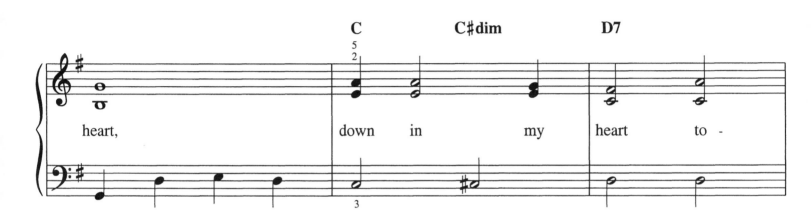

C   C#dim   D7

heart,   down   in   my   heart   to -

G   G7   C

day.   I've   got   that   peace   that   pass - eth

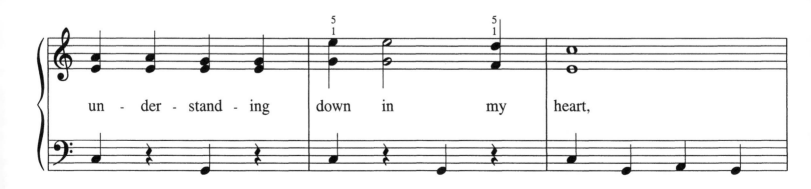

un - der - stand - ing   down   in   my   heart,

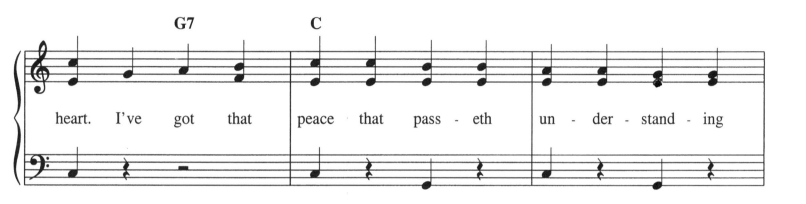

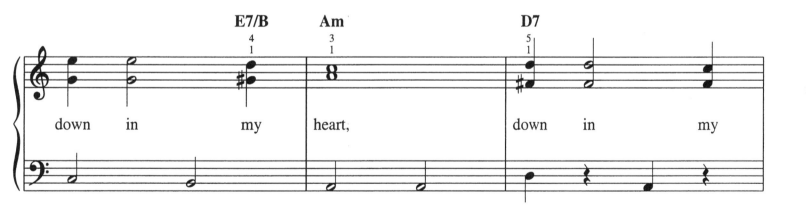

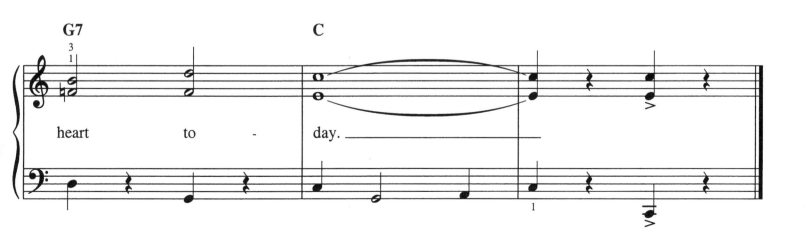

GIVE ME OIL IN MY LAMP

Traditional

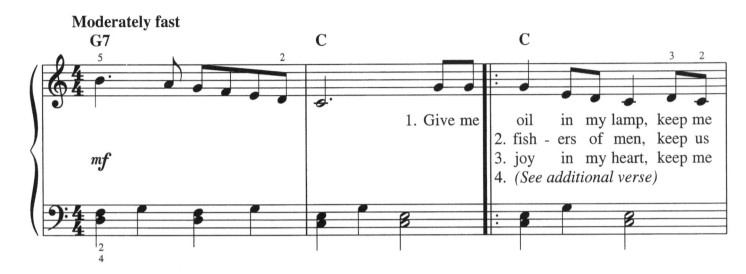

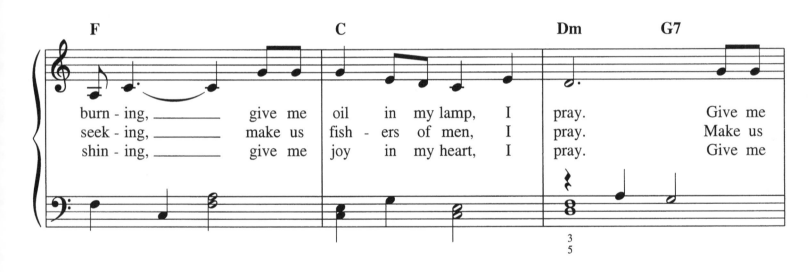

Additional Verse

4. Give me love in my soul,
   Keep me serving.
   Give me love in my soul,
   I pray.
   Give me love in my soul,
   Keep me serving.
   Keep me serving 'til the break of day.
   Chorus

GLORY BE TO GOD ON HIGH

Traditional

GOD IS SO GOOD

Traditional

Additional Verses

4. I'll do His will,
   I'll do His will,
   I'll do His will,
   He's so good to me.

5. Jesus is Lord,
   Jesus is Lord,
   Jesus is Lord,
   He's so good to me.

I AM A C-H-R-I-S-T-I-A-N

Traditional

HALLELU, HALLELUJAH!

Traditional

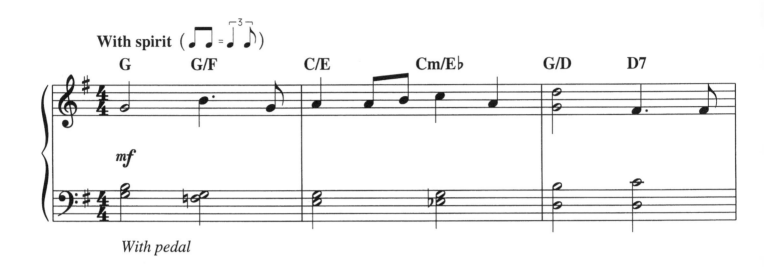

Hal - le - lu, hal - le - lu, hal - le - lu, hal - le - lu - jah,

praise ye the Lord. Hal - le - lu, hal - le - lu, hal - le -

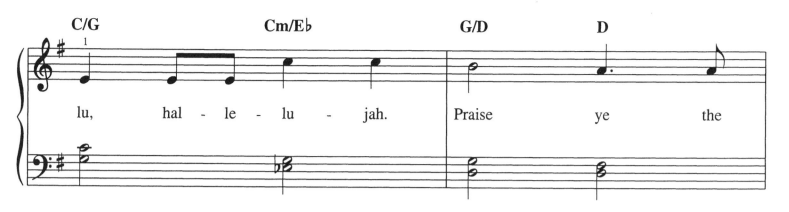

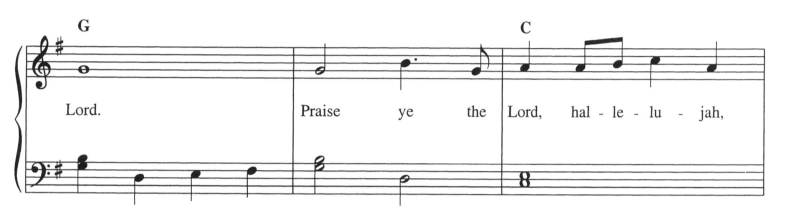

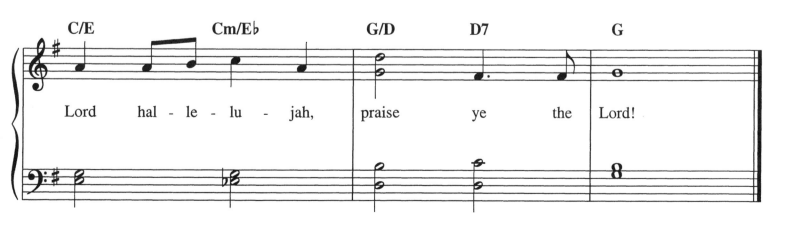

HIS BANNER OVER ME IS LOVE

Text based on Song Of Solomon 2:4, 16
Traditional Music

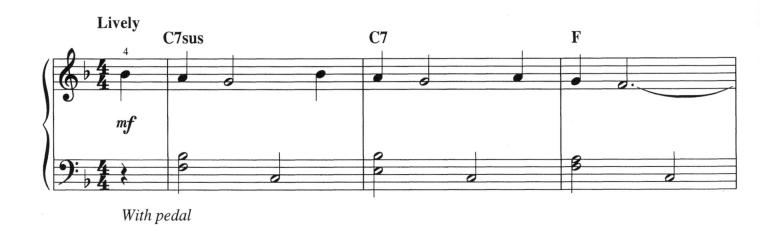

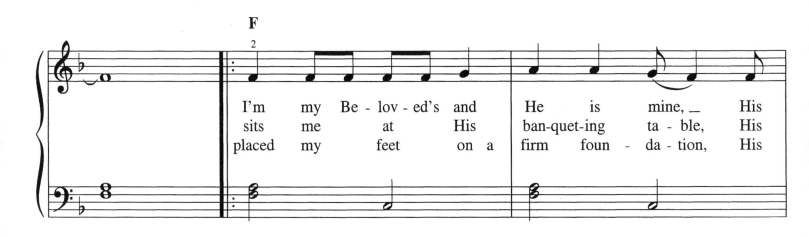

I'm my Be - lov - ed's and He is mine, __ His
sits me at His ban-quet-ing ta - ble, His
placed my feet on a firm foun - da - tion, His

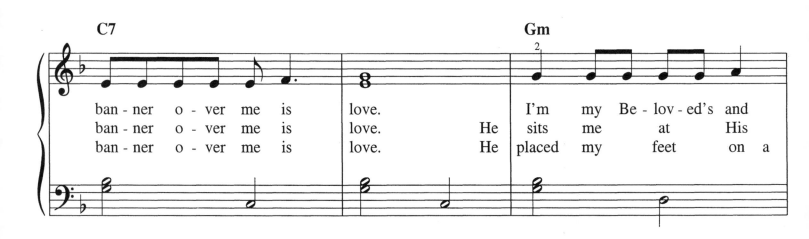

ban - ner o - ver me is love.
ban - ner o - ver me is love. He
ban - ner o - ver me is love. He

I'm my Be - lov - ed's and His
sits me at His
placed my feet on a

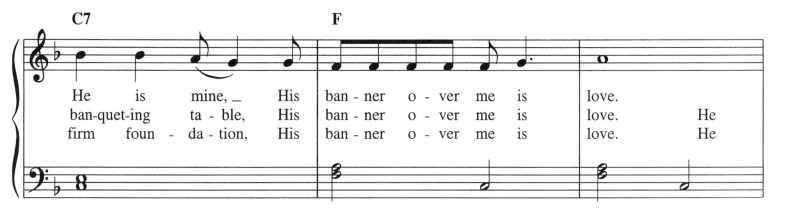

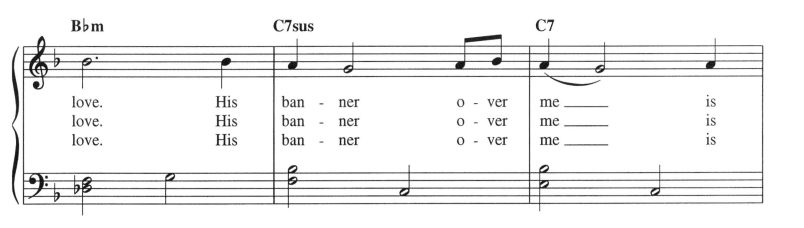

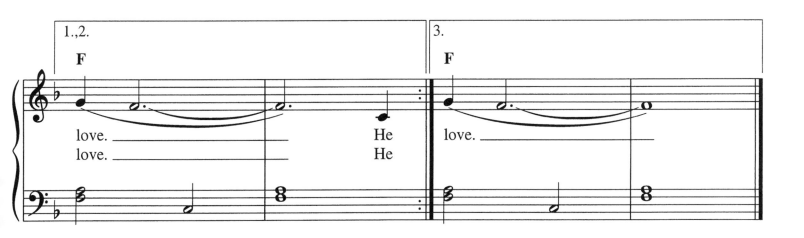

HO-HO-HO-HOSANNA

Traditional

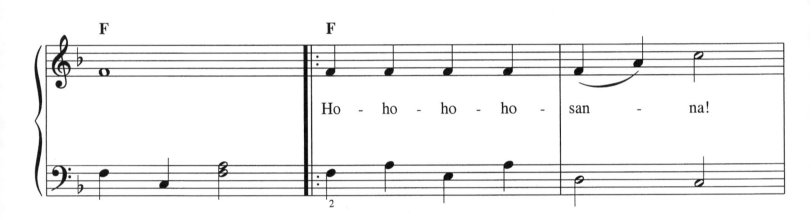

Ho - ho - ho - ho - san - na!

Ha - ha - hal - le - lu - jah!   He   He   He   He

I'LL BE A SUNBEAM

Words by NELLIE TALBOT
Music by EDWIN O. EXCELL

Moderately

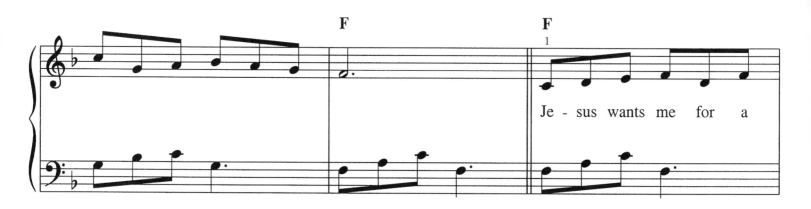

Je - sus wants me for a

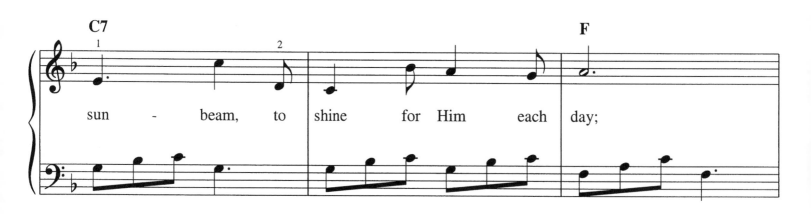

sun - beam, to shine for Him each day;

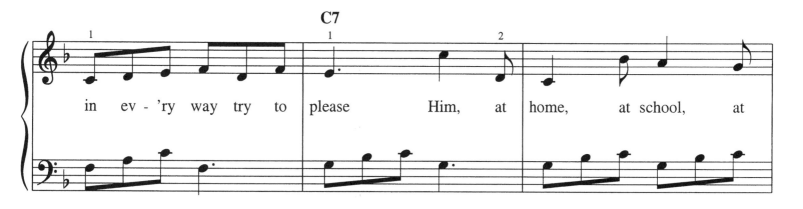

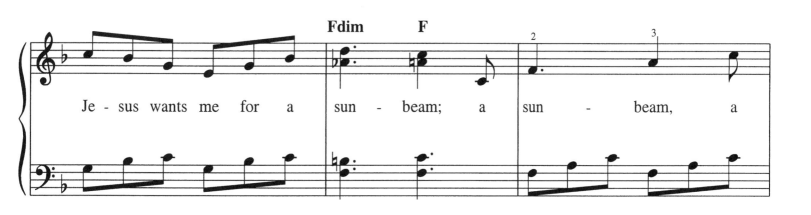

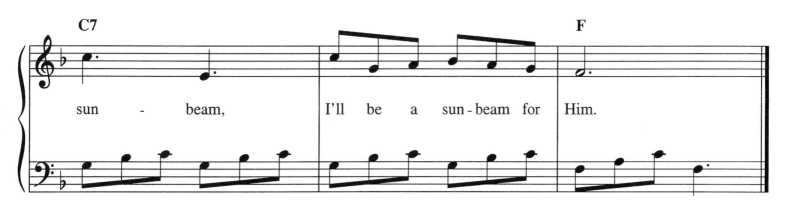

I'M GONNA SING
WHEN THE SPIRIT SAYS SING

Traditional Spiritual

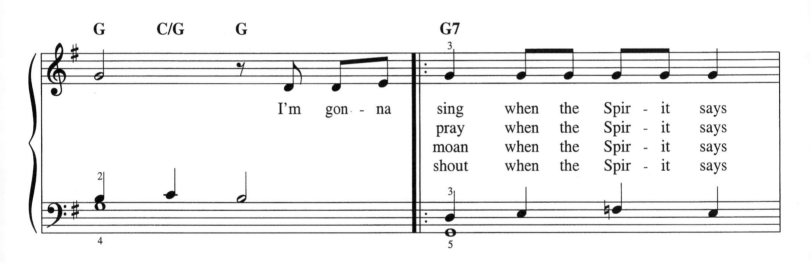

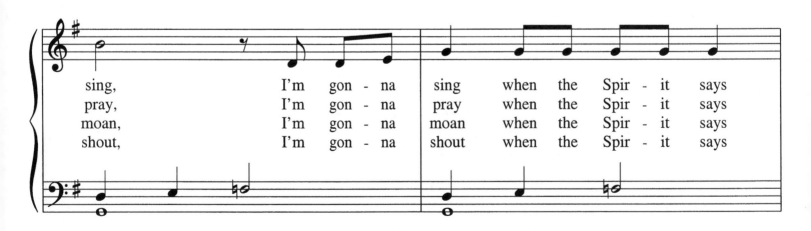

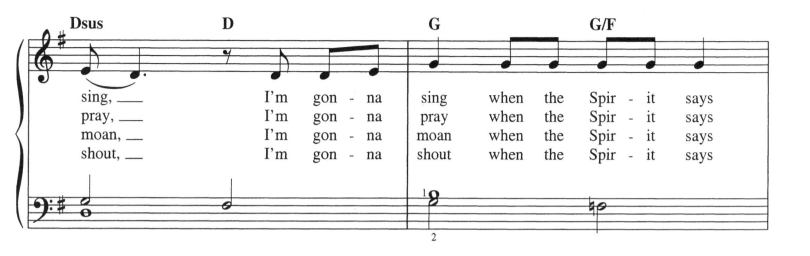

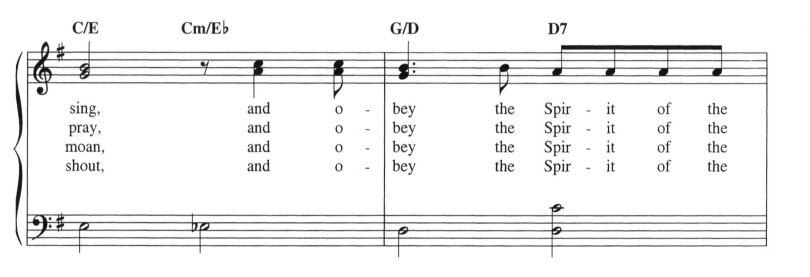

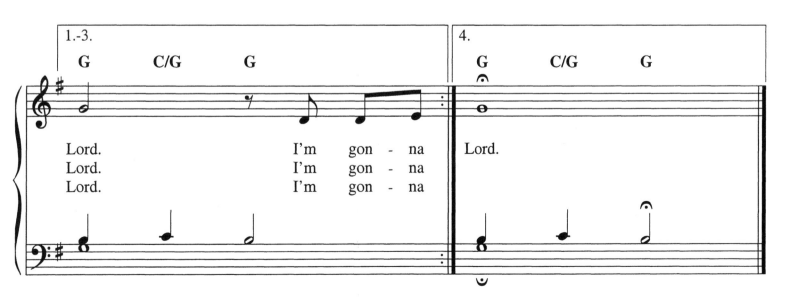

I'M IN THE LORD'S ARMY

Traditional

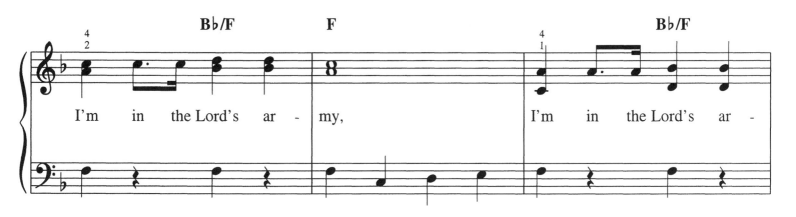

I'm in the Lord's ar - my, I'm in the Lord's ar -

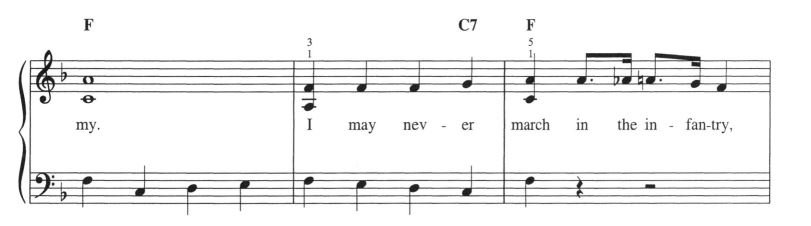

my. I may nev - er march in the in - fan-try,

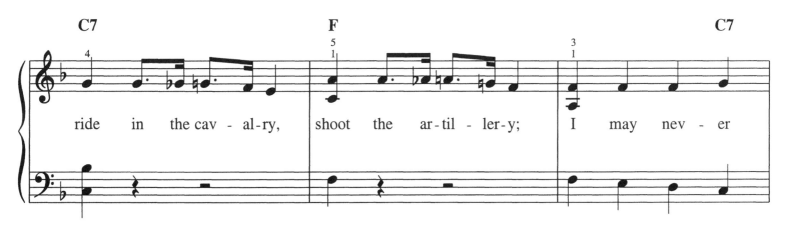

ride in the cav - al-ry, shoot the ar - til - ler-y; I may nev - er

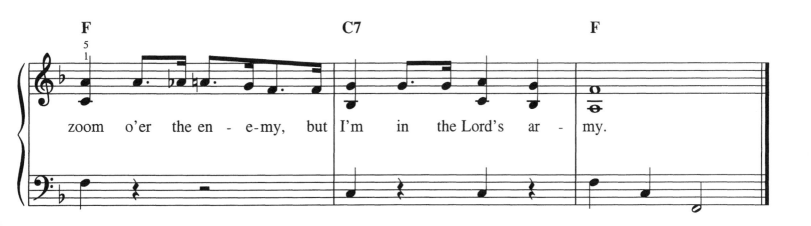

zoom o'er the en - e-my, but I'm in the Lord's ar - my.

I'VE GOT PEACE LIKE A RIVER

Traditional

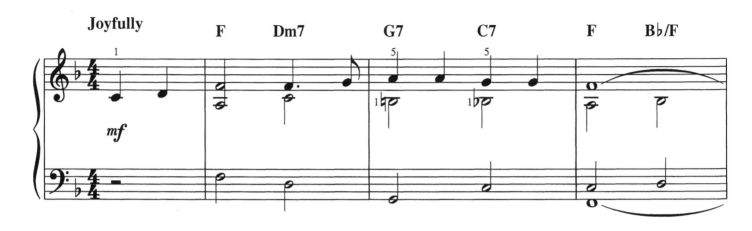

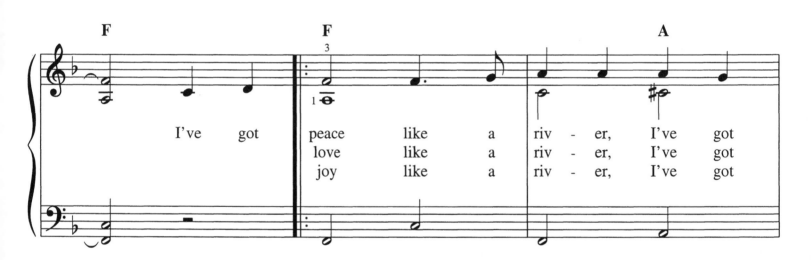

I've got | peace like a riv - er, I've got
love like a riv - er, I've got
joy like a riv - er, I've got

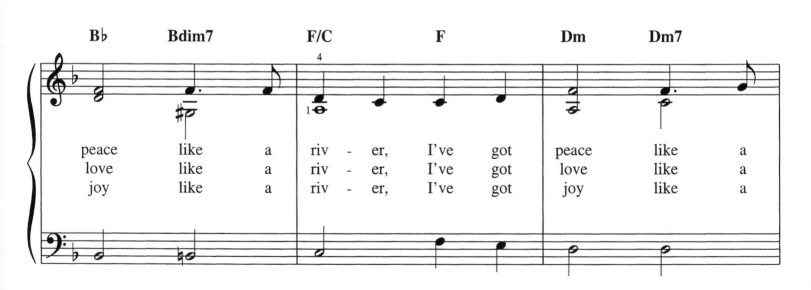

peace like a riv - er, I've got | peace like a
love like a riv - er, I've got | love like a
joy like a riv - er, I've got | joy like a

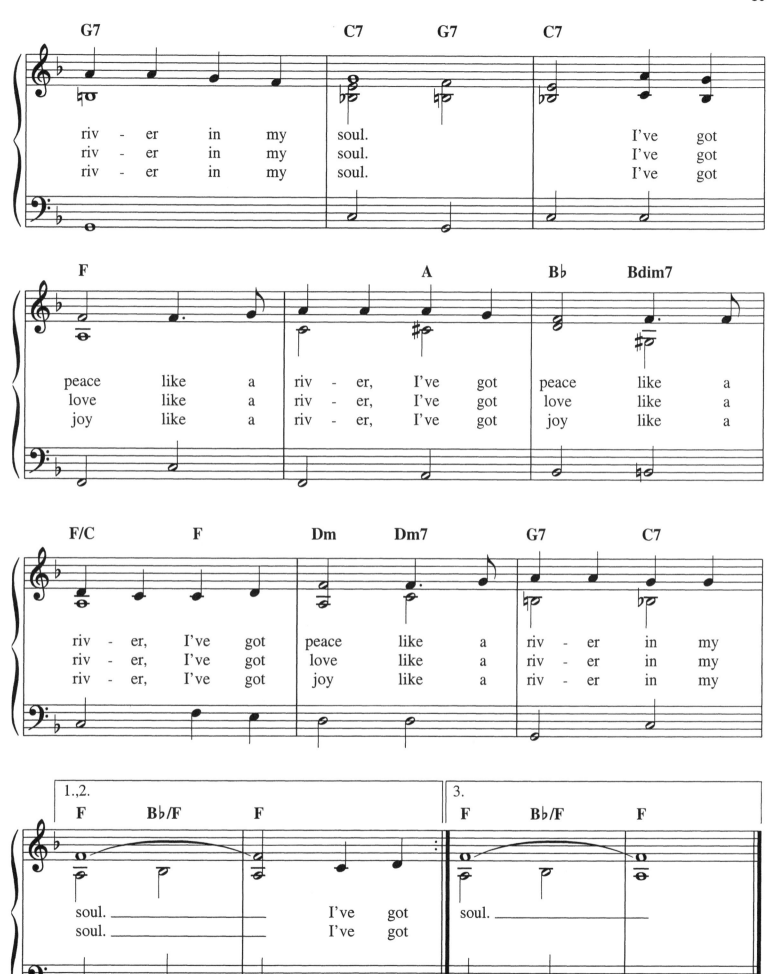

IF YOU'RE HAPPY AND YOU KNOW IT

Words and Music by
L. SMITH

JACOB'S LADDER

African-American Spiritual

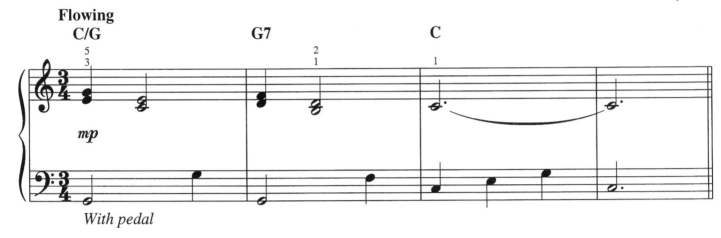

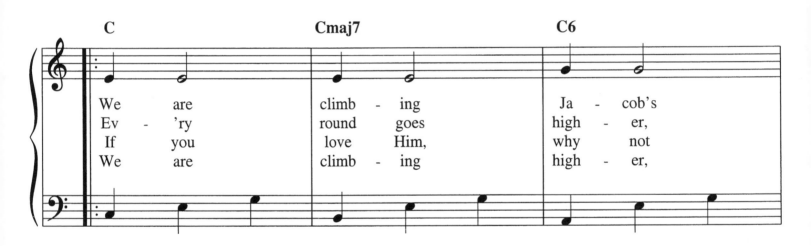

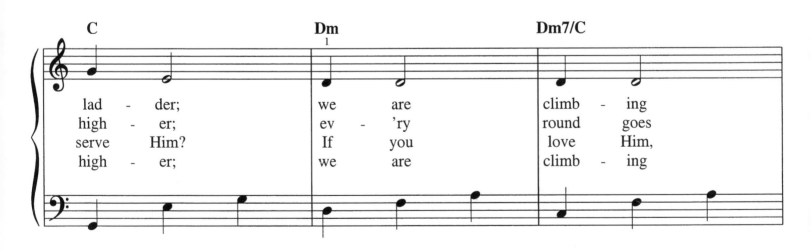

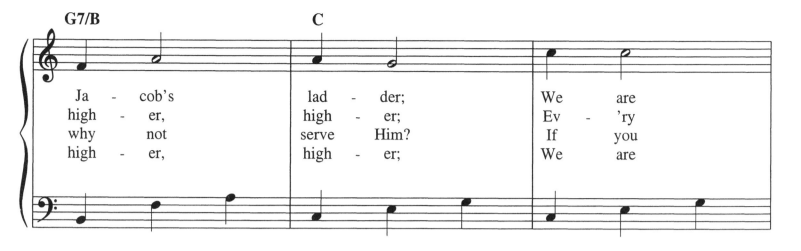

G7/B   **C**

Ja - cob's   lad - der;   We   are
high - er,   high - er;   Ev - 'ry
why   not   serve Him?   If   you
high - er,   high - er;   We   are

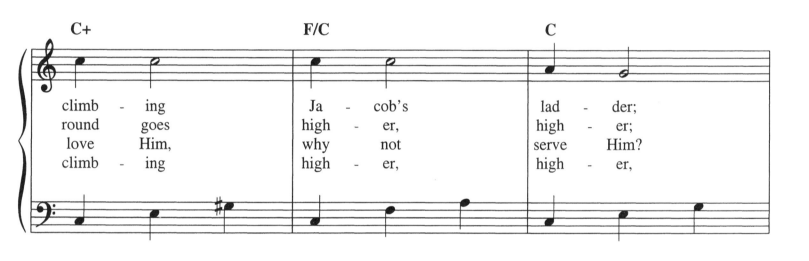

C+   **F/C**   **C**

climb - ing   Ja - cob's   lad - der;
round goes   high - er,   high - er;
love Him,   why   not   serve Him?
climb - ing   high - er,   high - er,

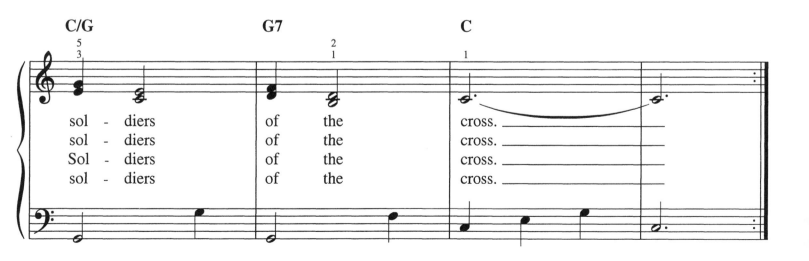

C/G   **G7**   **C**

sol - diers   of   the   cross. _____
sol - diers   of   the   cross. _____
Sol - diers   of   the   cross. _____
sol - diers   of   the   cross. _____

JESUS IN THE MORNING

Traditional

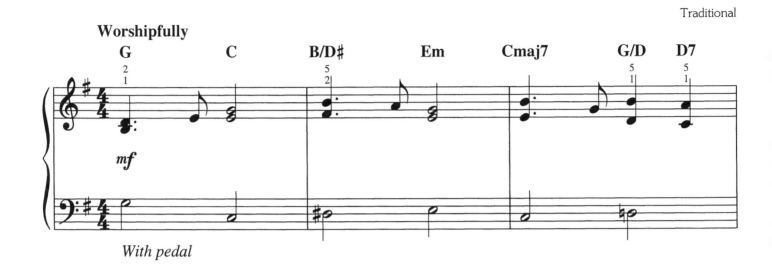

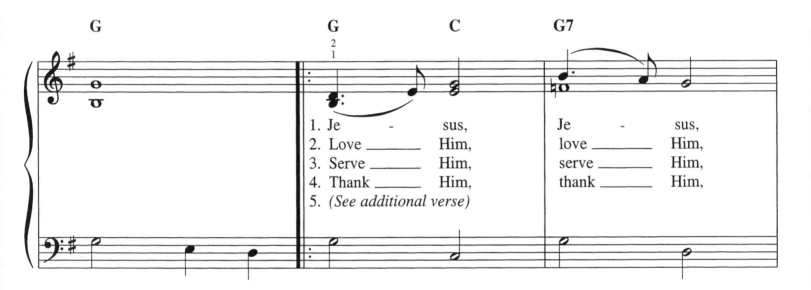

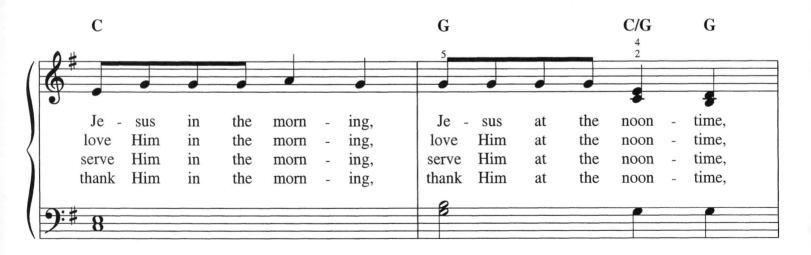

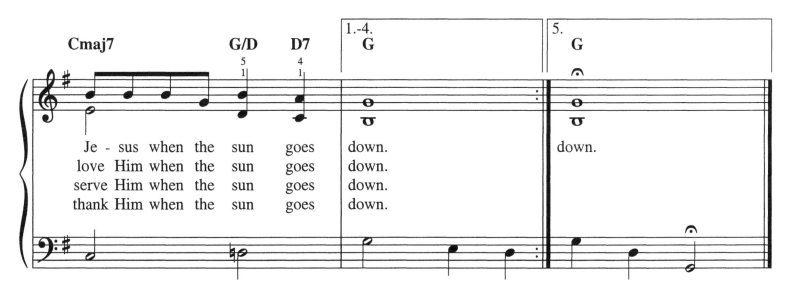

Additional Verse

5. Praise Him, praise Him,
   Praise Him in the morning,
   Praise Him at the noontime,
   Praise Him, praise Him,
   Praise Him when the sun goes down.

JESUS LOVES THE LITTLE CHILDREN

Words by REV. C.H. WOOLSTON
Music by GEORGE F. ROOT

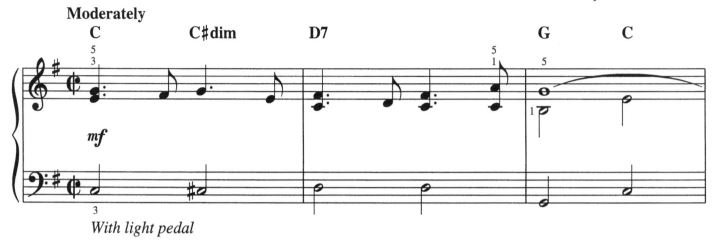

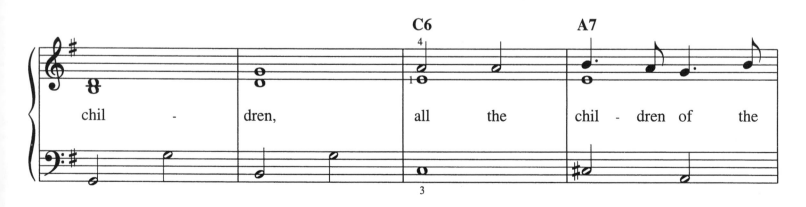

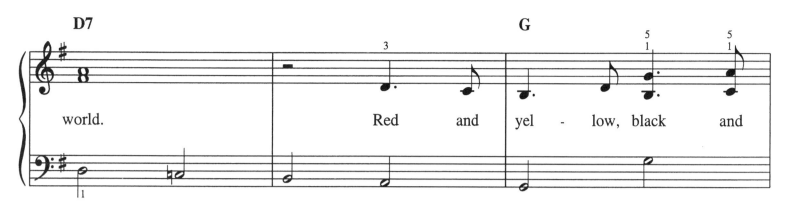

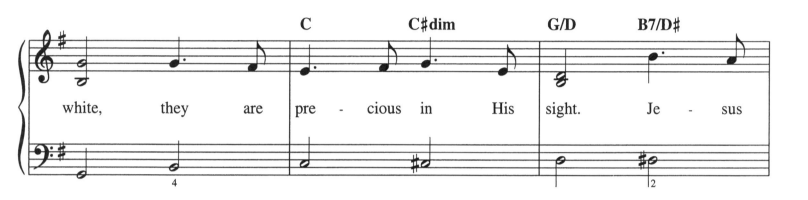

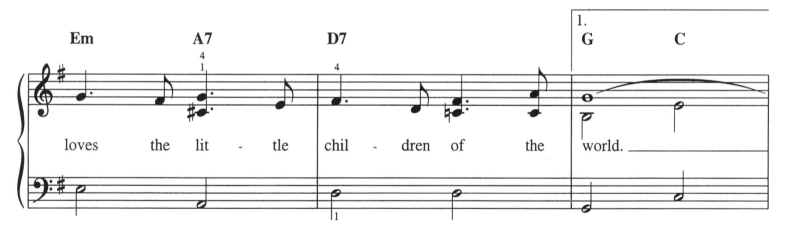

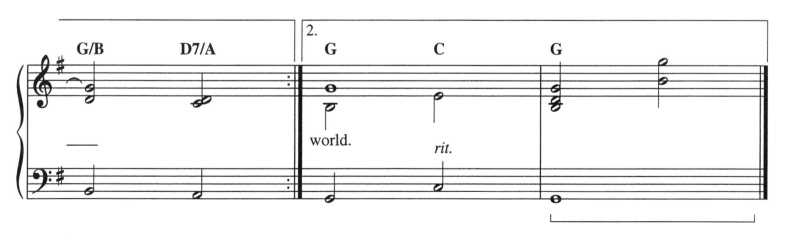

KUM BA YAH

Traditional

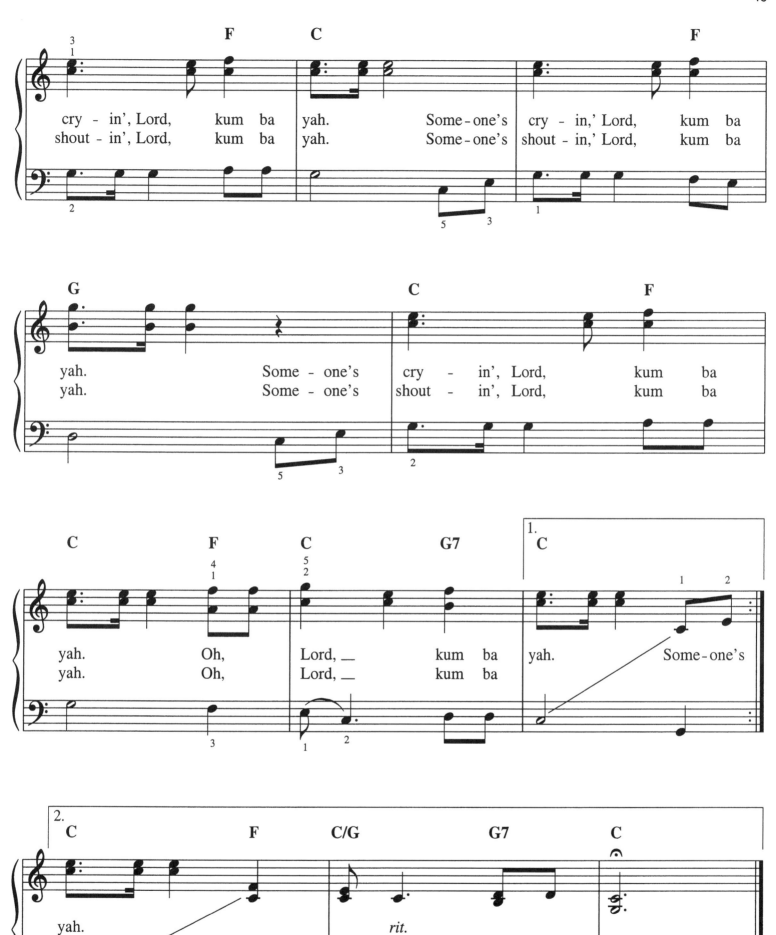

MY GOD IS SO GREAT, SO STRONG AND SO MIGHTY

Traditional

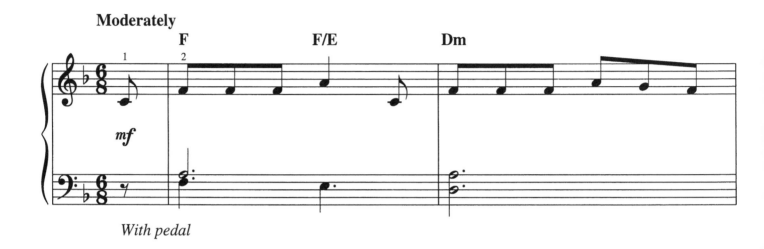

With pedal

My God is so great, so

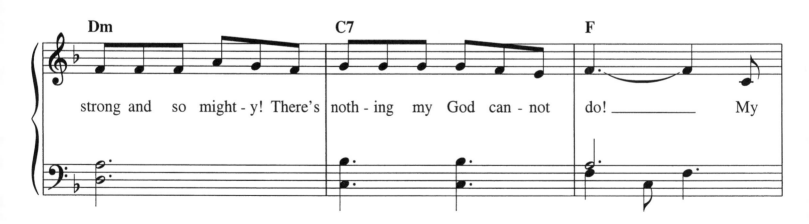

strong and so might-y! There's noth-ing my God can-not do! _____ My

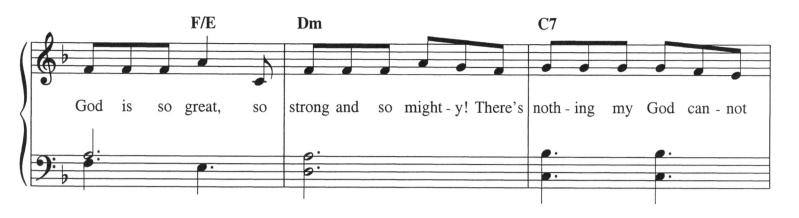

God is so great, so strong and so might-y! There's noth-ing my God can-not

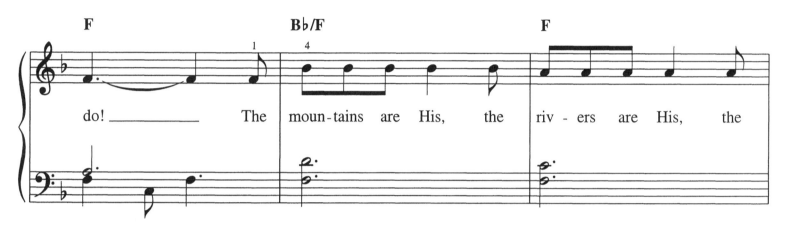

do! _____ The moun-tains are His, the riv-ers are His, the

stars are His hand-i-work, too. _____ My God is so great, so

strong and so might-y! There's noth-ing my God can-not do!

OH, HOW I LOVE JESUS

Words by FREDERICK WHITFIELD
Traditional American Melody

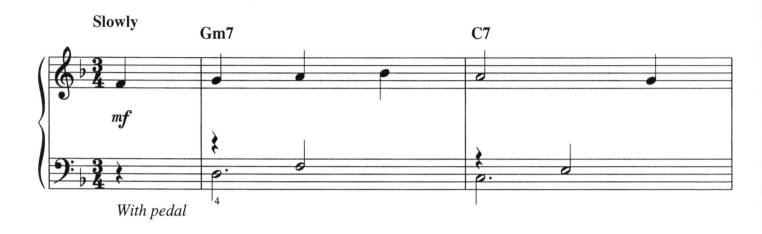

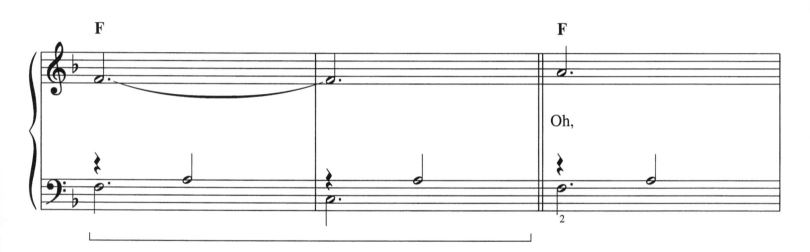

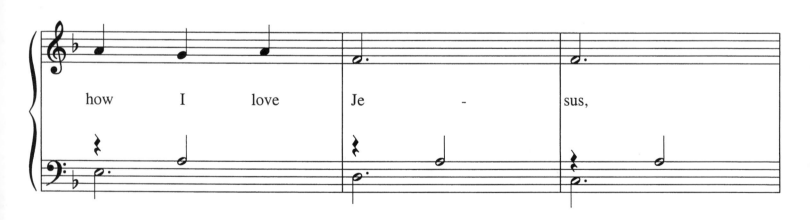

how I love Je - sus,

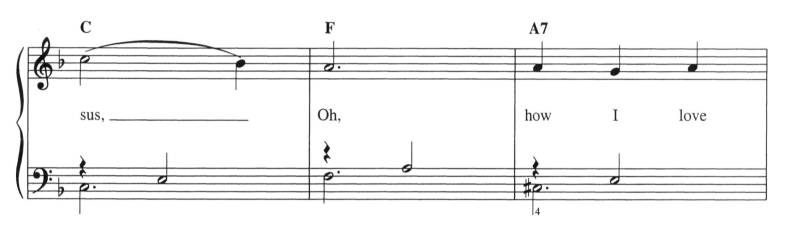

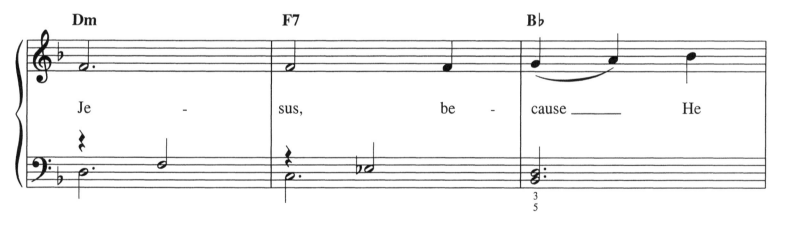

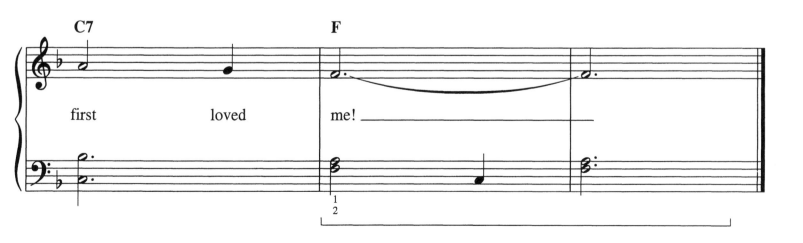

SIMPLE GIFTS

Traditional Shaker Hymn

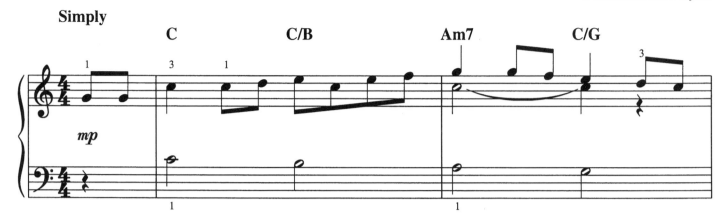

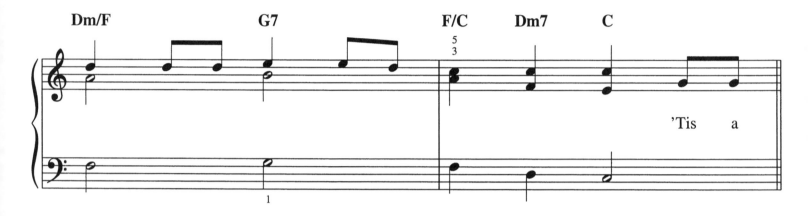

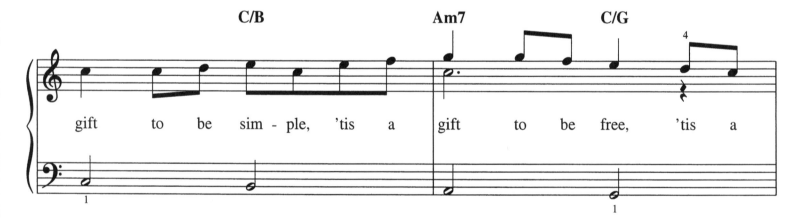

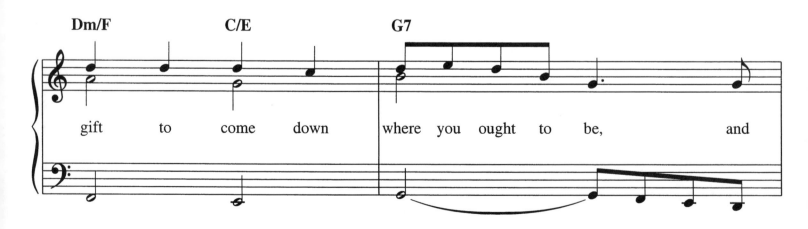

STOP! AND LET ME TELL YOU

Traditional

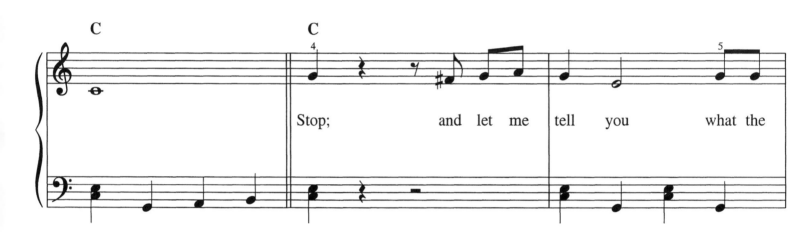

Stop; and let me tell you what the

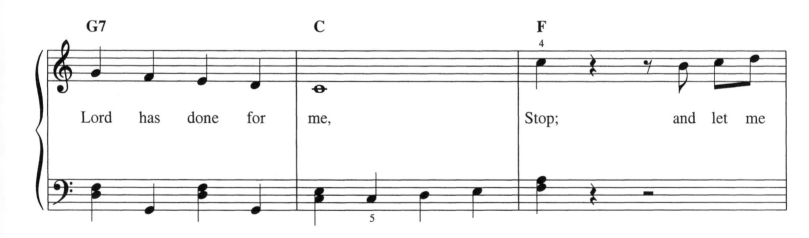

Lord has done for me, Stop; and let me

tell   you   what the   Lord   has   done   for

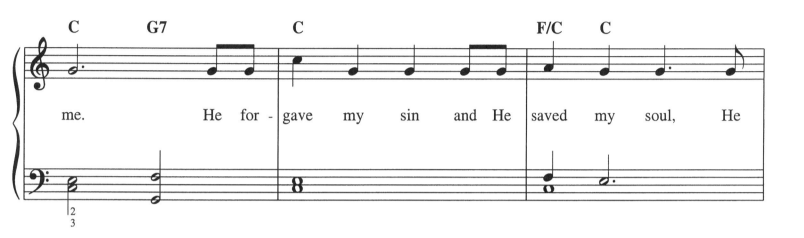

me.   He for - gave   my   sin   and He   saved   my   soul,   He

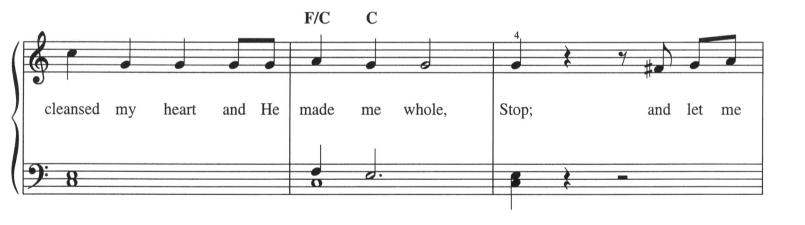

cleansed my   heart   and He   made   me   whole,   Stop;   and let me

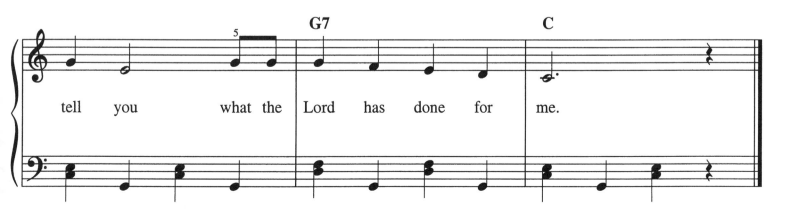

tell   you   what the   Lord   has   done   for   me.

TELL ME THE STORIES OF JESUS

Words by WILLIAM H. PARKER
Music by FREDERICK A. CHALLINOR

Flowing

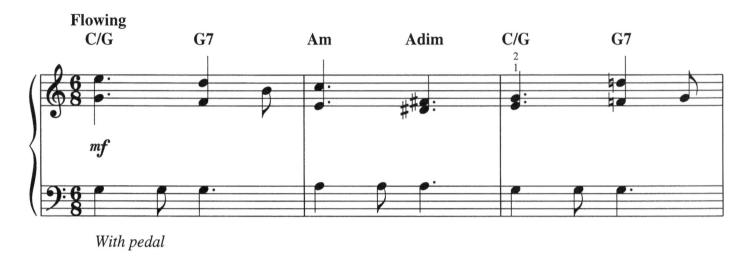

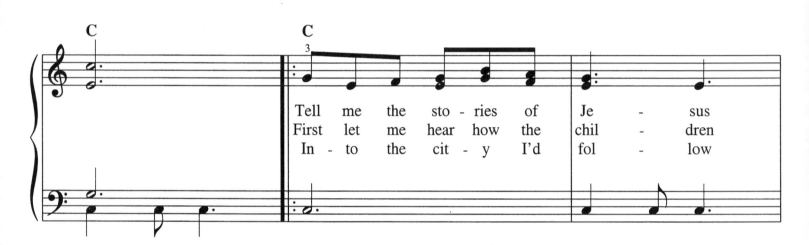

Tell me the sto - ries of Je - sus
First let me hear how the chil - dren
In - to the cit - y I'd fol - low

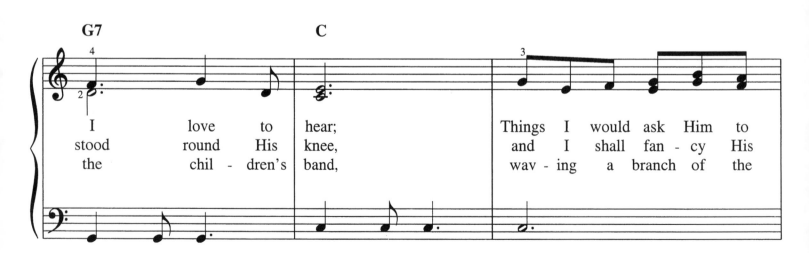

I love to hear;
stood round His knee,
the chil - dren's band,

Things I would ask Him to
and I shall fan - cy His
wav - ing a branch of the

THIS IS MY FATHER'S WORLD

Words by MALTBIE BABCOCK
Music by FRANKLIN L. SHEPPARD

Reverently

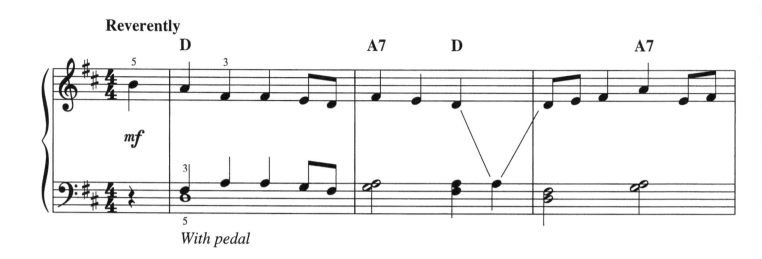

With pedal

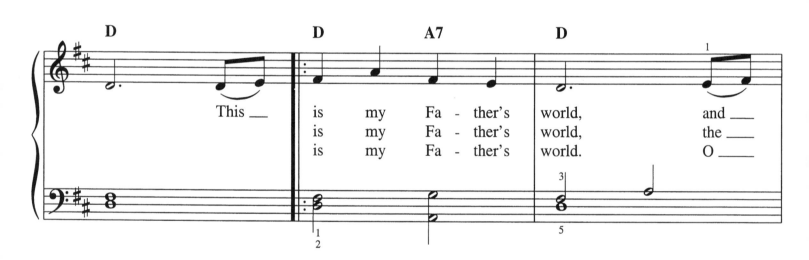

This ___ is my Fa - ther's world, and ___
is my Fa - ther's world, the ___
is my Fa - ther's world. O ___

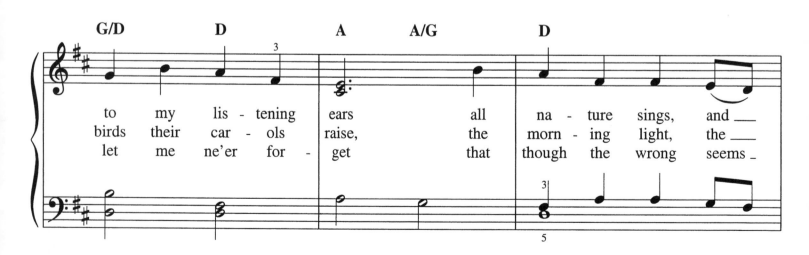

to my lis - tening ears all na - ture sings, and ___
birds their car - ols raise, the morn - ing light, the ___
let me ne'er for - get that though the wrong seems ___

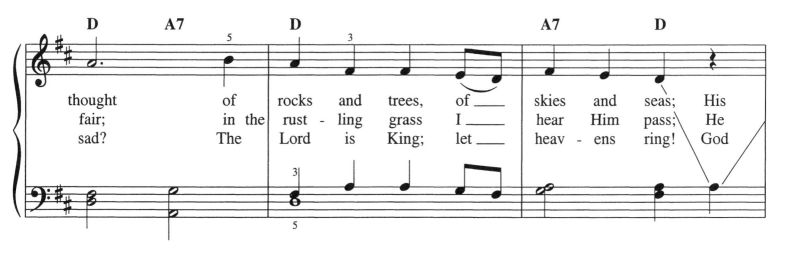

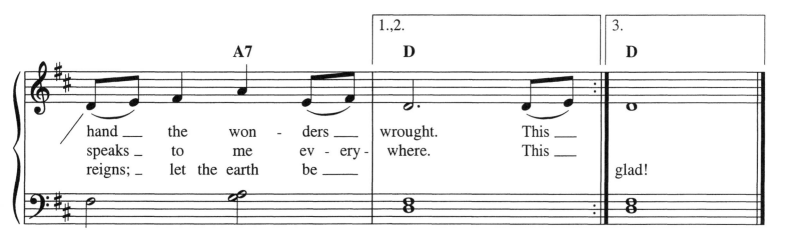

THIS LITTLE LIGHT OF MINE

African-American Spiritual

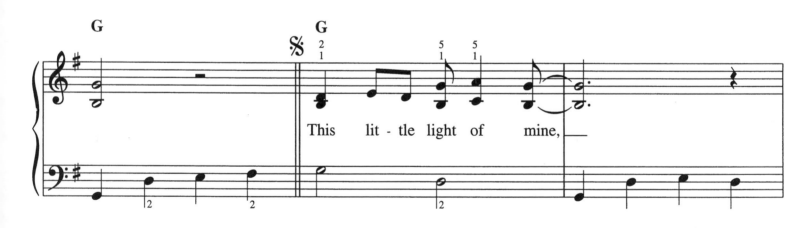

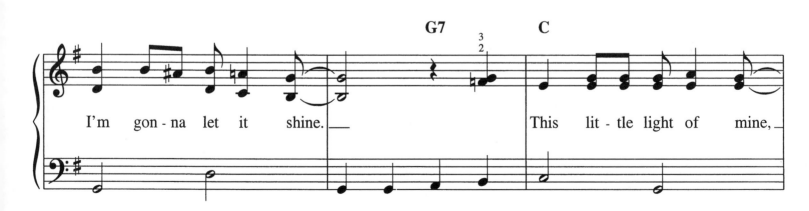

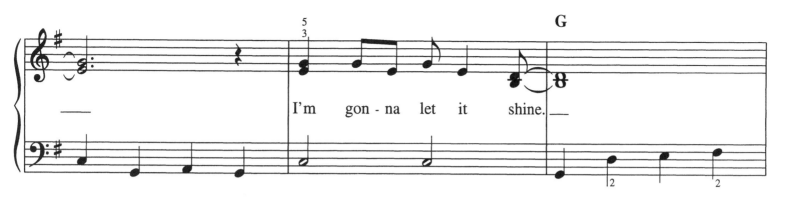

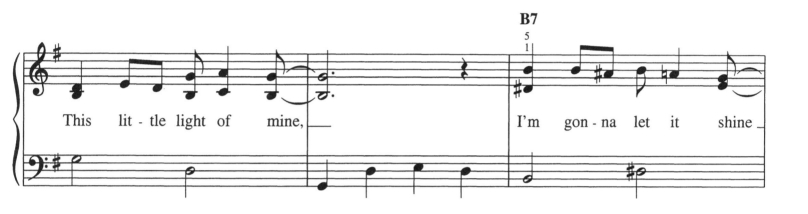

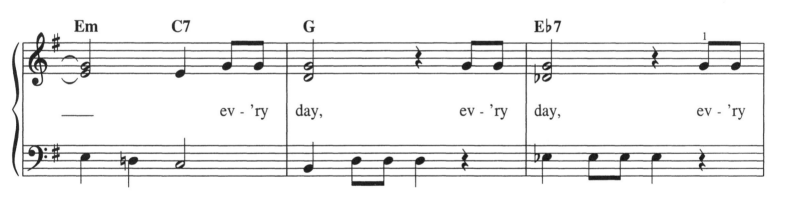

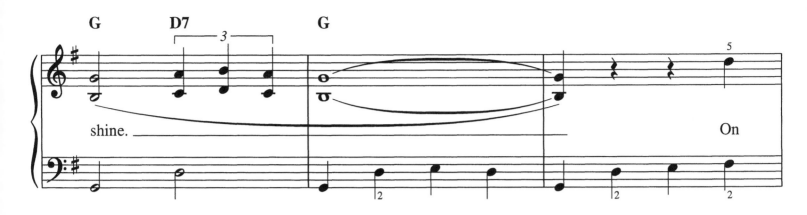

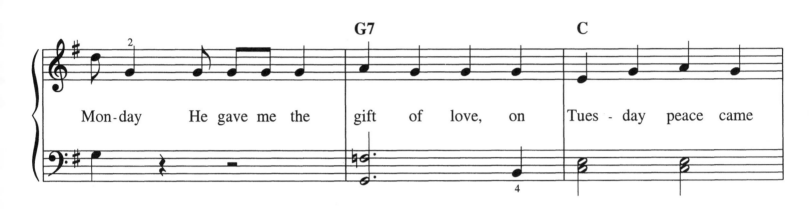

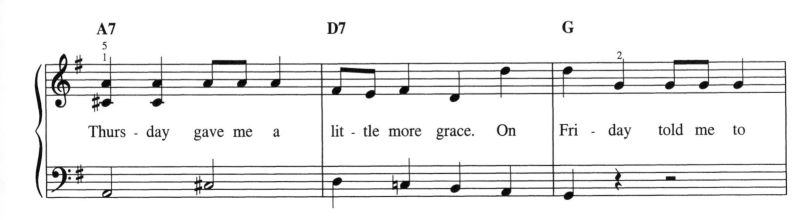

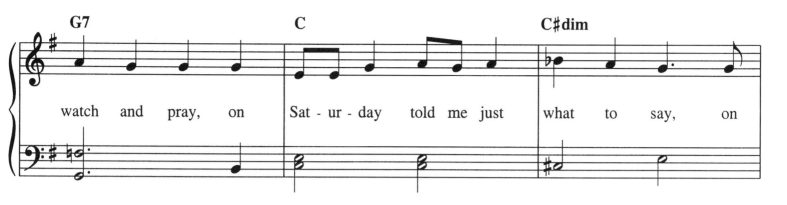

watch and pray, on Sat - ur - day told me just what to say, on

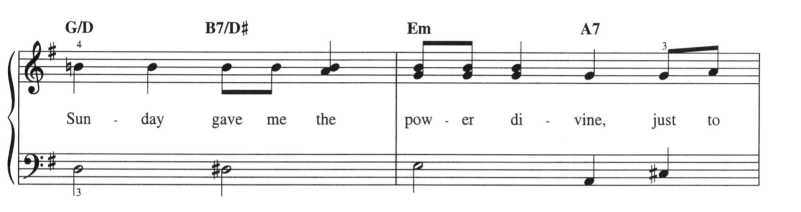

Sun - day gave me the pow - er di - vine, just to

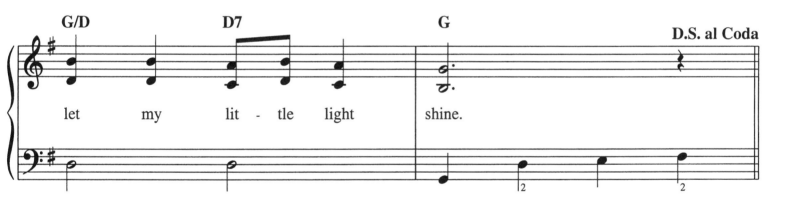

let my lit - tle light shine.

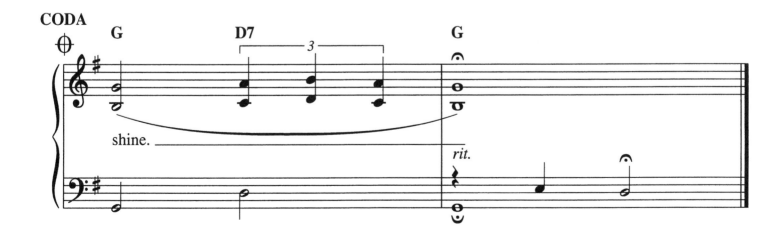

shine.

WHAT A MIGHTY GOD WE SERVE

Traditional

In a bright two

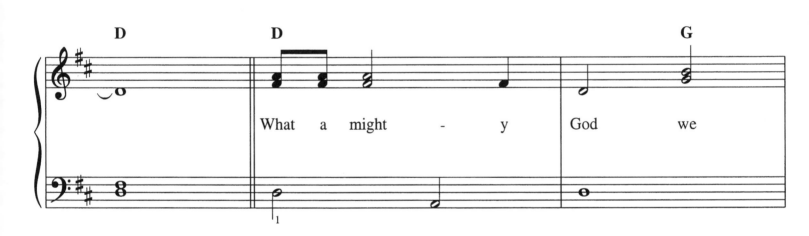

What a might - y God we

serve, _____ what a might - y

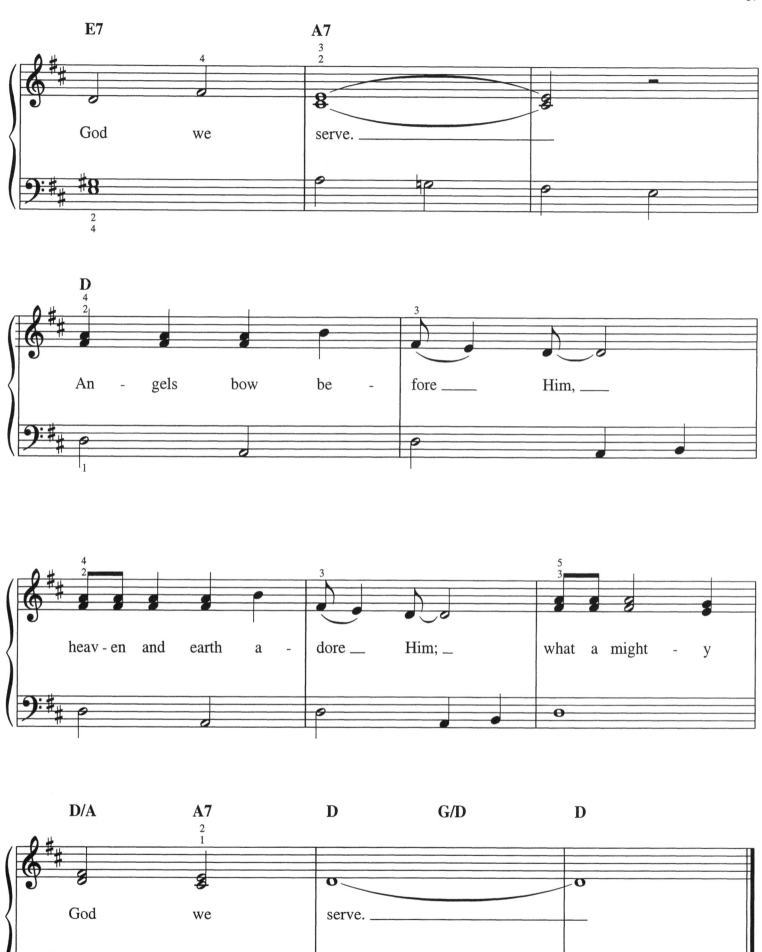

WHEN THE SAINTS GO MARCHING IN

Words by KATHERINE E. PURVIS
Music by JAMES M. BLACK

Bright Dixieland tempo

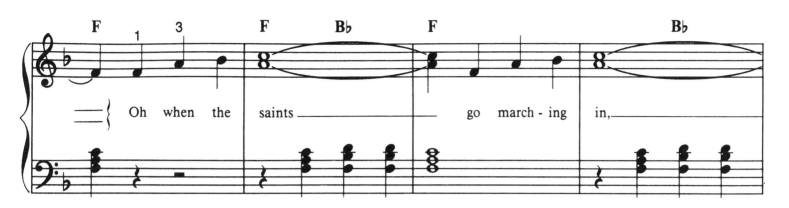

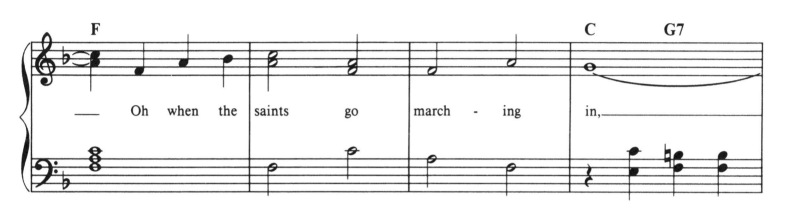

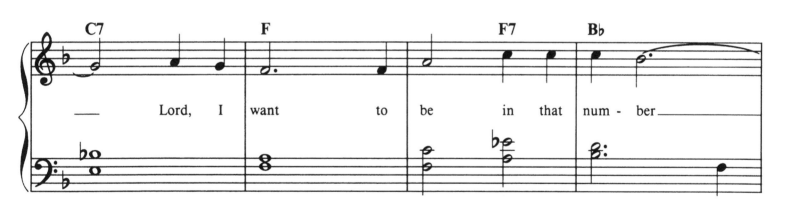

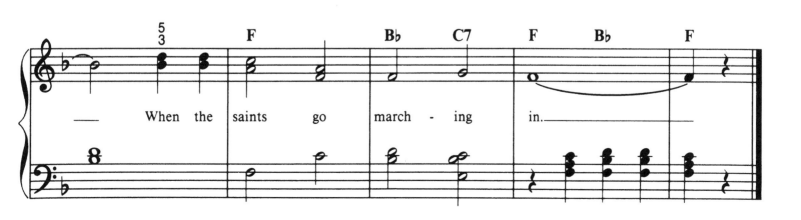

ZACCHAEUS WAS A WEE LITTLE MAN

Traditional

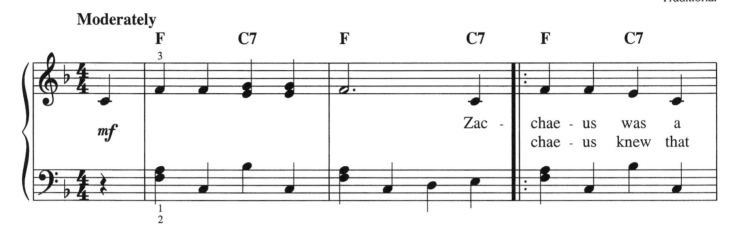

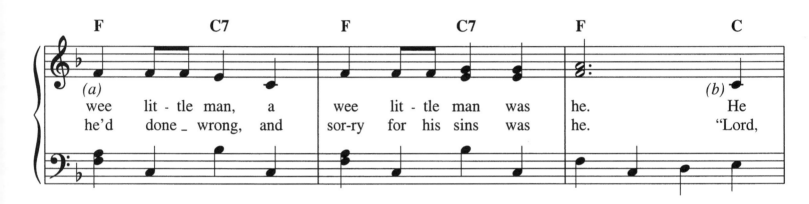

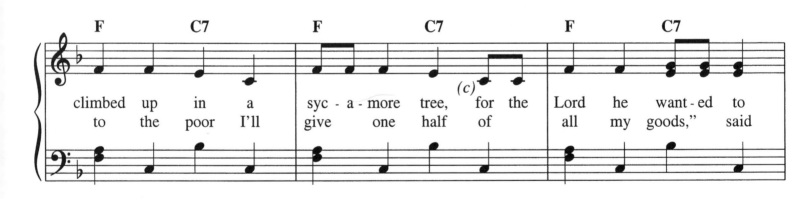

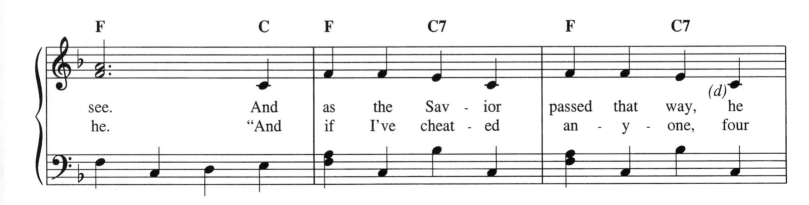

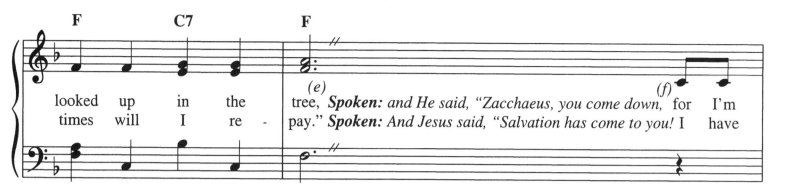

looked up in the tree, **Spoken:** *and He said, "Zacchaeus, you come down,* for I'm
times will I re - pay." **Spoken:** *And Jesus said, "Salvation has come to you! I* have

(e)
(f)

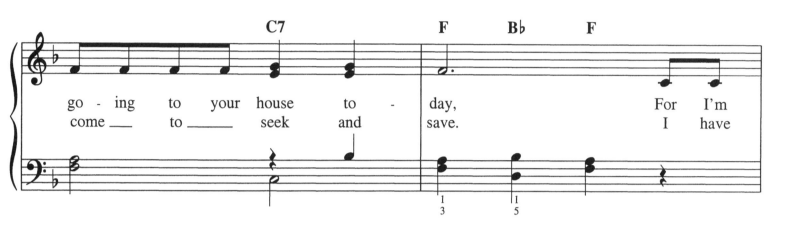

go - ing to your house to - day, For I'm
come ___ to ___ seek and save. I have

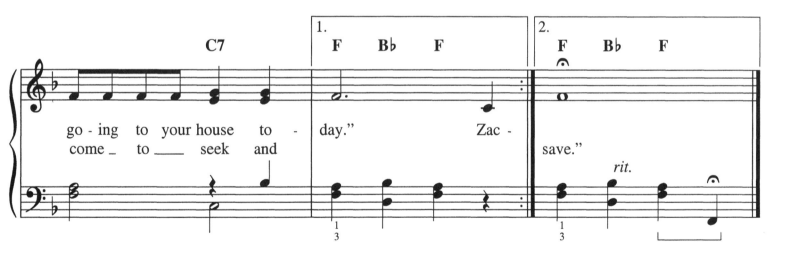

go - ing to your house to - day." Zac -
come _ to ___ seek and

day." save." *rit.*

Motions for Verse 1:

(a) *Hands in front, right palm raised above left palm.*
(b) *Alternate hands in climbing motion.*
(c) *Shade eyes with right hand and look down.*
(d) *Shade eyes with right hand and look up.*
(e) *Speak these words while looking up and beckoning with hand.*
(f) *Clap hands on beats 1 and 3 until end of Verse 1.*

PRAISE HIM,
ALL YE LITTLE CHILDREN

Anonymous Text
Music by CAREY BONNER